THE NONSENSE OF NEUTRONS

A drama

by

John Glass

☛ ☛

john@studentplays.org

Copyright information. Please read!

☞ About Student Plays ☜

Student Plays consists of **John Glass, Jackie Jernigan,** and **Dominic Torres.** We are a group of playwrights and directors that have written scripts for elementary school through college. We are proud of the variety of ages that our scripts serve.

Student Plays has "creepy" plays, and we also have Latino-themed plays. These are scripts that focus on Latino youths and the Latino experience. Any school can perform a Latino-themed play: it just requires a general introduction and basic exposure to the Spanish language, something that most schools and students already have.

To learn more, visit www.studentplays.org, or to contact one of the playwrights directly, simply email us at john@studentplays.org.

☆ Characters ☆

SHANNON	Twenties. Angry. Moody.
SETH	Late twenties/early thirties. Reserved. The "old man" of the group.
JACKIE	Twenties. Sarcastic. The youngest of the group.
THOMAS	Twenties. Loud, jokey, but moody. Struggles with his conscience.
DETECTIVE	Forties/Fifties. Any gender.

The setting is Bay State College, a small university in the Bay area. The time is the summer of 1995, the fifty-year anniversary of World War Two. The four main characters are all attending summer classes. Both SETH and THOMAS work in the campus café, and so in Scenes Two and Five they are wearing uniforms/shirts that designate this. Each scene can be a simple setup of tables and chairs.

Needs: Two "perukes," or powdered wigs, the kind used in the Revolutionary era. Fake cigarettes/joints.

Breakdown of Scenes

Scene One: A dorm room.

Scene Two: The campus café.

Scene Three: A patio table outside, near the campus courtyard.

Scene Four: A small room on campus.

Scene Five: A back-room or office of the café. There is a telephone on a small table and also a pay telephone.

SCENE ONE

At RISE: Nighttime, very late. A dorm room. All four characters are sitting around, hanging out, smoking a joint. The scene opens with JACKIE, exuberant, in the middle of telling a story. There are scattered books and a few backpacks.

SHANNON. He did *that??* Threw *firecrackers* . . . in the fire?

JACKIE Yeah! It was classic. It was a big Boy Scouts get-together, and they had this big bonfire going. And that idiot just walked over and threw a pack of M80's in there!

THOMAS What??

JACKIE *(Laughing even harder.)* Yes!! Right in the fire! And it just went BOOM!

SETH You date some questionable characters, Jackie.

JACKIE *Dated.* This was July 4th, two years ago. But it was hilarious! They all jumped back and just stared at him! It sounded like an atom bomb went off or something!

SHANNON It sounded like a *what*?

JACKIE An atomic bomb! An explosion!

(Beat. She stops and looks at SHANNON.)

You *know*. A bomb??

SHANNON I get it. An atomic bomb.

JACKIE Anyway, it was a riot. I wish you guys could have seen it.

SETH Damn.

THOMAS That's nuts.

JACKIE Well, My ex was nuts.

THOMAS So anyway, Seth, back to Lou. What does he want us to do?

SETH Well. We've got to have each corner of the ballroom marked off for certain historical characters.

JACKIE That dinner symposium thing? BOR-RING.

SETH It's gonna be a big deal. He wants one corner as the 'Roosevelt corner' and then another as the 'Harry Truman corner,' and so forth. And we also have to wear those historical wigs.

THOMAS The George Washington wigs?? Sweet!!

SETH Yep.

JACKIE A bunch of old military veterans, sitting around, talking about World War Two. Dumb.

SETH Hey, easy. Shannon's dad served in the war.

JACKIE Oh, right. Sorry.

SHANNON No, *dumb* is the right word.

THOMAS I don't think it's dumb. Fifty-year anniversary! Kind of cool. Plus, it'll be July the 4th weekend! Party!

SETH Yeah. Lou was telling me that Bay State had a hard time scheduling some of those guys. The elderly scientists that worked on the bomb. I guess they've been visiting different universities, for the anniversary. You know, delivering their speeches or papers.

SHANNON Their *papers*. Ughhhh.

SETH Yeah. Whatever they're called.

JACKIE Aren't those dudes all really old by now?

SHANNON Can we please stop talking about all this? About *history*? Between my roommate and all of the anniversary bullshit, it's all I hear. That, plus the weed.

THOMAS Ha! We know, Shannon. You're not very fond of the American past!

SHANNON I'm not very fond of a *lot* of things.

THOMAS But you sure as hell like to argue about it!

SHANNON Please. You heard about me arguing with *one* person. Over those stupid American flags.

JACKIE Who was it? Somebody in class?

SHANNON It was nobody. Somebody at some dumb party.

SETH That party at Josh's.

SHANNON Let's drop it, please.

SETH Has your roommate been at it again, Shannon? Getting all patriotic?

SHANNON God, you have no idea.

THOMAS What's up with her?

SHANNON She's in the ROTC, and they're doing that Enola Gay celebration next week.

JACKIE *Who's* gay?

SHANNON The Enola Gay. The plane.

SETH The plane that dropped the bomb over Japan.

JACKIE Oh.

SHANNON The ROTC is having some kind of anniversary celebration over it. Just like this symposium dinner.

JACKIE Lame.

SHANNON Anyway, yeah. She's been on the phone all week, yapping about it with her parents. I can't wait till that geek moves out.

JACKIE Ha, I bet. That girl *is* a geek.

SHANNON Oh, it's horrible.

SETH Hmmm.

(Beat. He checks his watch.)

Wow, it's getting late.

THOMAS What time is it?

SETH One thirty.

THOMAS Damn, it *is* late.

SETH *(Standing to leave.)* I guess I'm outta here.

JACKIE Does the old man have to go to bed?

SETH The old man has to work the breakfast shift in the morning.

THOMAS *(Also standing.)* You *and* me.

SHANNON *(Grabbing THOMAS's hand.)* You don't want to stay a little longer? Just for a bit?

JACKIE Yeah, come on. There's plenty of weed left.

SETH No thanks, I'm done. Gotta get up super-early. *(Leans down and gives SHANNON a quick kiss.)* Are you going to the library tomorrow?

SHANNON I'll be up there around three o' clock.

SETH All right. I'll come find you.

THOMAS Hey Shannon.

SHANNON Yeah?

THOMAS You *are* going out there, right? To get our little supply?

SHANNON Yes. I said that I was, didn't I?

THOMAS Are you sure?

SHANNON Are you deaf?

SETH Lay off, numb-nuts. She's going.

THOMAS I just need to be sure. Gotta plan my budget for this all-star pot.

JACKIE Hell yeah.

SHANNON *(To THOMAS.)* Are you sure you're cut out for it?

THOMAS Huh? Of course.

SHANNON Okay.

THOMAS Why wouldn't I be?

SHANNON Oh, who knows? With you, I never know. One day you're smoking weed. The next day, you're trying to quit.

SETH *(Exiting.)* Bro, you coming?

THOMAS Uh, yeah. *(Staring at SHANNON as he catches up with SETH.)* Right behind you.

SETH I'll talk to you tomorrow, Shannon. I'll bring those art history notes.

SHANNON Okay.

JACKIE Later, grandpa. Later, *grandpas*!

THOMAS Night.

(They exit. Pause as they smoke. Both of them are high so they speak slower. JACKIE holds the joint for the rest of this scene.)

JACKIE Wow. I haven't been this high in a long time. Almost a week, I think.

SHANNON Don't you have class in the morning?

JACKIE Yeah. But not until nine. Microbiology.

SHANNON Yuck. I have chemistry.

JACKIE Mmmm. I still can't believe I'm taking summer classes.

SHANNON Yeah.

JACKIE But it sure beats spending the summer in Ohio. Want to hit this again?

SHANNON No, I'm fine. *(Pause. She leans back and stretches, very high.)* I've kind of got a headache.

JACKIE You know, I hate that you have to go to Humboldt alone. Can't you just go the *next* week? I can go with you then.

SHANNON My connection can only meet me on the third for the price we're getting.

JACKIE Weird. That's a Friday, right?

SHANNON Yes. Same day as that dumb history dinner thing. I'm gonna drive up there that day, then go visit my cousin.

JACKIE In Arcata?

SHANNON Yep. Haven't seen her in years. I'll be back on Saturday.

JACKIE July 4th.

SHANNON Yep.

JACKIE In time for the weekend! Can't wait. Totally can't wait.

(Beat.)

Um . . . so . . . how is he?

SHANNON How is who?

JACKIE You know . . . Seth.

(Pause.)

SHANNON He's good. Um. We've been hanging out quite a bit.

JACKIE I wouldn't call three or four months simply *hanging out.* I see how much you two are together.

SHANNON Well. Yeah. I think . . . I think he's good for me.

JACKIE Oh.
(Beat.)
So . . . that's it?

SHANNON Yeah . . . he's a solid guy. He really is.

JACKIE Oh.

(JACKIE starts to cough. It worsens, and she holds her hand up.)

SHANNON Hey, are you okay? Do you need water?

(The cough gets worse. JACKIE is red-faced, and looks desperate. SHANNON gets up and rushes to her, whacks her on the back.)

SHANNON Jackie?? Stand up! *(She leans down to her.)* JACKIE!!

(After a few seconds JACKIE smiles and bursts into laughter.)

JACKIE Ha ha, I got you, girl!

SHANNON Oh, you little . . .

JACKIE That was priceless!

SHANNON *(Quietly, as she sits back down.)* I'm gonna get you. You wait . . .

JACKIE You should have seen your face!

SHANNON Well. Revenge is sweet. Never forget that.

JACKIE Oh, that was good! Now you know not to be elusive with me when I ask you a personal question!

SHANNON Whatever.

JACKIE *(Still laughing.)* Oh, man. Sorry!

SHANNON Forget it.

JACKIE Wow . . .

(Beat. She collects herself.)

So . . . um. Tell me. What was Thomas talking about earlier? What did you do with those American flags?

SHANNON It was at a party. They were bothering me. So I ripped them up.

JACKIE Ha! Girl, you trip me out. Just like that?

SHANNON Just like that. I was actually alone when I did it. Outside on a back patio. But then some guy walked out and saw me doing it and wanted to argue about it.

JACKIE Wow.

SHANNON Yep. Stupid flags.

JACKIE But . . . your father once saluted the American flag. Didn't he?

SHANNON Um.

JACKIE *(Giggling, lost in being high, and in her joke.)* What would he say about what you did? If he found out?

SHANNON Um. He really can't *say* anything.

JACKIE *(Giggling very hard.)* Girl, he would totally disown you!!

SHANNON Yeah. Maybe.

JACKIE He would!

(Pause. More laughter. SHANNON closes her eyes, puts her fingertips to her temples, increasingly very high.)

JACKIE *(Gradually calming down.)* Oh man. That's as funny as hell.

SHANNON Yep . . .

JACKIE Are you . . . okay?

SHANNON I don't know . . .

JACKIE How many joints have you smoked? Two??

SHANNON Yeah.

JACKIE That's it? Oh my God, I'm hanging out with a two-joint pansy!

SHANNON Excuse me??

JACKIE You know. Two beers and two joints and you're already out of it . . .?

SHANNON Well . . . maybe . . . *(Explosively.)* Maybe that's just the WAY THAT I AM!! OKAY???

(She stands at stares down at JACKIE, who is mortified. Long pause.)

SHANNON GOT IT?

(Another pause. SHANNON snickers, then slowly sits down.)

SHANNON Got you.

JACKIE Oh, shit . . . what are you DOING?? You scared me!!

SHANNON Revenge, princess. I told you. It's all about revenge.

JACKIE Apparently!

SHANNON What goes around come around.

JACKIE *(Gets ahold of herself.)* Man. I'll get you. When you least expect it.

SHANNON I'll be waiting.

JACKIE You really did get me!!

SHANNON Yep.

JACKIE That was convincing, girl. Ha.

SHANNON I'm all about paying people back.

JACKIE Paybacks, indeed. Wheww. *(Looking through her backpack.)* I swear I could get high all night. Do you have any more papers?

SHANNON Papers? For the pot?

JACKIE Yeah.

SHANNON No. *(Beat. She slowly digs out a pack of papers from her backpack.)* Oh, wait. Hang on. Yeah. Here. Here they are . . .

JACKIE *(Taking the papers, begins to roll a joint.)* Ah-hah. I thought you had some.

SHANNON *(Scoffing.) Papers*. I'd like to get my hands on those papers.

JACKIE Huh?

SHANNON You know . . . those old guys at that symposium thing. Delivering their papers. Their speeches on World War Two.

JACKIE Oh.

SHANNON Their papers on protons and neutrons. *(Pause.)* The nonsense of neutrons, my mother used to always say.

JACKIE *(High and confused.)* Whaa . . .?

SHANNON Am I speaking Yiddish? The neutrons. You know.

JACKIE Okay. Um. Whatever.

SHANNON Yep. I'd like to get those papers. I definitely would. And then . . . I'd like to do something else.

(She leans her head back, pulls her hair back slowly. She is very high. JACKIE just stares at her while continuing to roll the joint. Lights fade to black.)

SCENE TWO

At RISE: The campus restaurant/diner. A few days later, just after lunch. SETH and THOMAS are working, wiping down tables, etc. THOMAS is wearing a white wig, the kind used in a typical George Washington costume.

THOMAS Dude, I'm telling you. It was a scientist named Leo Sczilard.

SETH You're crazy. It was Oppenheimer.

THOMAS No it wasn't.

SETH Yes. It. Was. I remember that crap from my freshman year. It was Oppenheimer. *(Looks at his wig and laughs.)* Will you take that ridiculous thing off??

THOMAS No way, this is my getup. Come on, we gotta get in the spirit. And it was *Leo Sczilard*! He's probably going to give a speech at that dinner so he can tell you himself.

SETH Whatever. *Leo Sczilard.* Never heard of him. *(Sits down, rests.)* You look like a moron with that thing on.

THOMAS Don't let Lou hear you talking like that. He's all about this stuff.

SETH Lou knows where he can stick it.

(Pause. THOMAS continues to clean up while SETH remains seated.)

THOMAS So, dude. Are we all set? Is Shannon still going out there next week? For our weed?

SETH I believe so. I haven't talked to her about it in a few days.

THOMAS She's really been on edge. She didn't sound very pumped about going.

SETH Relax. She's going.

THOMAS Okay. Just checking.

SETH You sure have, uh, been hitting the weed hard.

THOMAS Huh? Not really.

SETH Come on. I see you every day. Aren't you trying to ease up some?

THOMAS Don't nag.

SETH Only asking.

THOMAS You sound like my mother.

SETH Well. Okay. But . . . isn't she part of the reason that you're—

THOMAS *(Flatly.)* Yes. She is.

SETH Okay.

THOMAS So . . . I hear you. I know.

SETH Sorry.

(Pause.)

THOMAS I mean . . . I *do* want to dial it back some. I just don't know . . . *how* to.

SETH Yeah.

THOMAS So . . . you know the deal.

(Beat. He looks down at a table.)

Ugh. All these nasty coffee spills.

SETH It's those professors that sit in here for hours and hours.

THOMAS Sheesh.

(Beat.)

Hey, so tell me. What the hell happened yesterday? Did Shannon really almost throw coffee on an old man at the diner?

SETH Um. It was pretty bad.

THOMAS Jimmy was there, he told me. Were they arguing over World War Two?

SETH Yeah. With Shannon, what else would it be? She overheard this guy in the booth behind us talking about Normandy. I think he actually *served* in Normandy. And then she turned around and decided to challenge him on it.

THOMAS Man!

SETH I had to pull her out of there. It was wild. And this old dude was no slouch.

THOMAS No way.

SETH Oh yeah. He was giving it right back to her.

THOMAS Wow.

SETH Yep.

THOMAS Dude . . .? I have to ask you: are you falling for her?

SETH I don't know.

THOMAS Sure seems like it.

SETH I'm trying to be there for her. You know . . .

THOMAS I'd say that you're doing more than just being there for her.

SETH Well, yeah, we've become pretty close. Her father isn't doing any better. And it's really got her down.

(Beat. Looking both ways to be sure they're still alone.)

Careful. She's supposed to drop by here and say hello.

THOMAS It's not an insurance thing, is it? He should have full medical coverage, from the military.

SETH No, it's not that. It's his mind. It's something mental.

THOMAS Oh. I kinda wondered what it was.

SETH Apparently the war really messed him up. And it really began to happen only about ten years ago. That's all she'll tell me.

THOMAS Wow. That's interesting.

SETH And it just eats at Shannon. Really bad. She carries it like a heavy burden. She just . . . *carries* it.

THOMAS Dang. That's interesting.

SETH You know a little something about that. About carrying burdens.

THOMAS Yes, I do.

SETH Your mother and all her drama.

THOMAS Well. *Our* drama.

SETH. Mhmm. Hey, remember to wipe down those chairs.

THOMAS *(Doing so.)* Yep. I know.

(Enter SHANNON, carrying a few books.)

SETH Lou will be saying that we aren't thorough.

THOMAS Again: Lou knows where he can stick it. *(Sees SHANNON.)* Well, damnation. There's the girl we want to see!

SHANNON I thought I'd find you two in here.

SETH Hey. We just finished with the lunch crowd. This place was a disaster.

SHANNON Oh.

SETH Are you headed to that tutoring thing?

SHANNON Yes. I shouldn't be gone too long.

THOMAS So Shannon, o queen, we were just talking about you.

SHANNON Hmm . . ?

THOMAS O queen with the lovely red Buick.

SETH Oh Lord . . .

SHANNON What is it?

THOMAS You *are* going to Humboldt, right? Next Friday? To get our little supply?

SHANNON *(With major irritation.)* Is that all you guys are going to talk about all summer? The great *Humboldt weed?*

THOMAS Sorry.

SETH I told him you were going to get it.

THOMAS No you didn't!

SHANNON *(Sarcastically and agitated.)* Yes, yes, yes! I am going to get the world's *best* marijuana!

THOMAS Hooray!

SHANNON Are you satisfied, Thomas?

THOMAS Just wanted to be sure!

SHANNON Damn . . .

THOMAS Oh, and hey, settle something for us really quick. During World War Two, which scientist had the original idea for the atomic bomb?

SETH Not now, dude!

THOMAS Oppenheimer or Leo Sczilard?

SHANNON Sczilard.

THOMAS *(To SETH)* Ha! Told you!

SETH Hang on, maybe she's wrong.

SHANNON No. I'm right. It was Sczilard.

THOMAS See? I told you she knew her American history.

SETH Dude, can you chill?

THOMAS Well, it's true. She knows all those obscure facts!

SHANNON Would you SHUT THE HELL UP?

THOMAS Whoa! I'm just kidding around. Not a big deal.

SHANNON With you, it's *never* a big deal until it's a *big deal!*

THOMAS Well, excuse the hell outta me!

SHANNON Don't you have dishes to take away? Pots to scrub?

THOMAS Well, as a matter of fact I do. *(Exiting with a tray of dishes.)* Man! Who bit your head off??

(Exits quickly.)

SHANNON Damn . . .!

SETH You can't let him bother you like that.

SHANNON I know it. But I *just* walked in here and he's already driving me crazy!

SETH Here, sit down for a minute.

(She grunts in disgust as he pulls over a chair. She sits down slowly, stressed.)

SETH What's up? You ok?

SHANNON Oh, I'm a wreck. An absolute wreck.

SETH You gotta stop worrying about everything.

SHANNON I know . . . I know. Look at this. *(She pulls out a postcard, hands it to him.)* A postcard from my mom. About my dad.

SETH *(Skimming over it.)* Wow. Man.

SHANNON He's much worse. She mailed that to me days ago. But she's called me twice since she mailed it.

SETH You need to go see him.

SHANNON I know. I've already decided. *(Pause.)* My father means the world to me, Seth. He means *everything.* There just are no words for our relationship.

SETH Then go! Don't let this dumb Humboldt trip get in the way. That weed can wait.

SHANNON I'm going after I get back. My mom really wants me to come home.

SETH Why don't you just go now?

SHANNON I can't . . .

SETH Why??

SHANNON It's not just the weed. It's everything. My chemistry exam. My microeconomics quiz. Driving up to Humboldt. My cousin.

SETH Humboldt can wait!

SHANNON No. July 3rd is the only day they can meet me. And I've already arranged to meet my cousin up there. That same day.

SETH But your father—

SHANNON *(Suddenly.)* Oh, Seth, stop! Please! I don't want to talk about it! I'll go see my father *after* next week! I just can't go home right now.

SETH *(Hugging her, consoling her.)* Sorry . . . I'll stop pushing.

SHANNON There's just too much going on right now. I'm gonna go see him the second I get back.

(Pause.)

SETH Okay. Well. We're still gonna hang out later, right?

SHANNON Yes. I've got that scary movie. Friday the 13th. Part 80.

SETH Good, ha. *(Laughing.)* We're gonna watch it on your beat-up VCR?

SHANNON Ha. Yes. It finally works. Just have to give it a little bang.

(Beat. Pulls him closer.)

Hey.

SETH Yeah?

SHANNON Do you know how much I've appreciated being around you lately?

SETH Uh. Yeah, I think.

SHANNON I'm so glad you didn't go back to Fresno for the summer. I hope you know that.

SETH Yeah.

SHANNON You've made the summer worthwhile.

SETH Well . . .

SHANNON *(Gives him a quick kiss, brushes fingers over his eyelids.)* Mmmm. You and these two North Stars.

SETH *(Embarrassed by her tenderness.)* Um. Not that again.

SHANNON It's true. The sky may have only one North Star . . . *(Still playing with his eyelids.)* . . . but I have two that I can look at. Right here.

SETH *(Further embarrassed.)* I don't have words for this. Um. I don't have anything.

SHANNON Yes you do . . .

SETH Mmm. So . . .

SHANNON *(Smiling)* So . . .

SETH We, uh, just gotta give your VCR a little bang, huh?

SHANNON That's right. A little bang.

SETH Ha.

(Enter THOMAS, carrying a tray.)

SHANNON I'd like to give that old man at the diner a little bang. Right across his head.

THOMAS Hey Shannon, here's one for you: where in New Mexico was the atomic bomb first tested?

SETH Bro, QUIT with the trivia!

SHANNON *Please* quit.

THOMAS Come on, where was it??

SHANNON Here's one for *you:* why don't you go work on your church boy routine??

THOMAS What??

SHANNON *(Exploding.)* Aren't you frightened to death of going into rehab?

THOMAS Huh??

SHANNON Aren't you?? It's stupid, the way you talk sometimes. *(Mimicking him.)* "Guys, do you think that we'll *always* smoke pot?" "Oh, if my mother knew I was still getting high it would crush her!"

THOMAS Where the hell's this coming from?

SHANNON Where the hell is your *face* coming from?

SETH Shannon!

THOMAS *(Sharply.)* Watch it.

SHANNON You think I'm scared of you? I once slapped a security guard! You don't frighten me!

THOMAS Is this really how you feel?

SHANNON Yes, it is!! And relax: nothing's changed. I'll go and get your stupid weed. But maybe you'll learn to chill with all the jokes.

THOMAS All I was doing was asking you a trivia question!

SHANNON About *history*! About World War Two! Which you know I get sick of talking about!! *(Begins to exit.)* I'll see you later, Seth.

SETH You're leaving??

SHANNON I've got to go tutor.

SETH You just got here!

SHANNON I'm taking off. I'll call you later.

SETH Okay. Sheesh. Bye . . .

SHANNON Bye, babe.

(She exits abruptly. Pause. They are both floored. THOMAS is very quiet and moody. SETH gradually returns to work in order to break the tension.)

THOMAS What the hell . . .?

SETH Yeah, I know that sometimes you can rattle her cage. But . . .

THOMAS She had to go *there*, didn't she?

SETH Well. Yeah.

THOMAS I know that she was pissed . . . but she had to go *there.* Damn.

SETH Makes you wonder what this trip to Humboldt is doing to us.

(Beat.)

I'll talk to her, man. It's her father. She's all stressed out over him.

THOMAS I'm gonna clock out, dude.

SETH Are you?

THOMAS Can you finish up by yourself? I don't feel very well.

SETH Yeah. I guess so.

THOMAS Thanks. I'll talk to you later, man.

(He starts to exit. SETH suddenly grabs the wig, tries to humor him.)

SETH Hey Thomas.

THOMAS What?

SETH I'm Georgie! You know . . .?

THOMAS I get it . . .

SETH George Washington . . .?

THOMAS I told you. I get it.

SETH Okay.

THOMAS Later.

SETH I'll talk to you later, man.

(Exit Seth. Pause. THOMAS looks around, picks up a tray/cleaning rag, and begins to work. Lights slowly fade.)

SCENE THREE

At RISE: A few days later, at a patio table, outside. JACKIE and SETH have just finished counting a large stack of money. JACKIE's backpack is lying on the table. A few coffee cups and an ashtray are also on the table.

JACKIE Are you sure that's it? Count it again.

SETH No, that's it. I counted it twice.

JACKIE Okay.

SETH Two hundred bucks.

JACKIE Okay. Good.

SETH *(Puts money in an envelope, sticks it in his pocket.)* Thomas is only putting in twenty-five. You know that, right?

JACKIE Yes. That idiot. Oh well, less weed for him, more for us. Cool, make sure that Shannon gets that money.

SETH Why *wouldn't* she get it?

JACKIE Oh, I don't know.

SETH Silly.

JACKIE I just wanna be sure she can buy the full amount. I'm *ready* for that pot!

(Beat.)

So, don't you have to be in the ballroom? Tonight's the big night, right?

SETH Yeah. About to leave.

JACKIE *(Sarcastically.)* Gonna decorate for the founding fathers?

SETH Yep. We start at four. Gonna be a long night.

JACKIE Oh. Well. I've got a date.

SETH No way.

JACKIE Some guy I met on that computer chat-room thing.

SETH Lord. I heard about that thing.

JACKIE Can you imagine . . .? Meeting a guy on the *computer?*

(Enter THOMAS, shaken, angry.)

SETH That thing's a dumb idea, if you ask me.

JACKIE Well, I fell for it.

SETH He'll probably have two heads.

THOMAS Seth, your girlfriend needs to be committed!! Seriously!

SETH Now what happened?

JACKIE What are you talking about?

THOMAS We just got into it again.

SETH Where?

THOMAS Out in the courtyard. Shannon's out there, yelling at this group of families for veterans or something.

SETH Agghh! Not again!

JACKIE I saw them. That group of families and students?

THOMAS I watched the whole thing. She walked right up and challenged them over their banner. She grabbed it!

JACKIE Yep. That big banner. What did it say? *God Bless the USA . . ?*

THOMAS Something like "God Bless our Families and Veterans." I don't know. But she got all in their faces about it. So I walked over and defended them. I'm tired of her shouting everybody down.

SETH Dude, why do you bother??

THOMAS No. No more. I can't just sit by and not do anything.

SETH It's been a long summer for her, Thomas.

THOMAS It's been a long summer for *all* of us! She's not the only one taking classes!

JACKIE She actually grabbed their banner?

THOMAS Yes! With both hands!

SETH Oh, God. Ughhh.

THOMAS *(Catching his breath.)* What time is it? We've got to put on those costumes for work.

SETH About 3:45. We've got a few minutes.

THOMAS Sheesh. *(Takes a breath.)* I don't feel like going in there and hearing Lou's voice. Even if we are getting paid time and a half.

SETH Well, get ready. He's all giddy because he got to meet a few of the scientists.

JACKIE Those scientist dudes are already here?

THOMAS Of course they're here! It's tonight!

JACKIE Don't bite *my* head off!

(Beat.)

And Thomas, where the hell's the rest of your money for the weed?

THOMAS I gave you guys my money.

JACKIE Twenty-five dollars? I thought you wanted to really score big on this stuff!

(Enter SHANNON, carrying backpack, very angry.)

THOMAS Mind your own business! You guys received my share, and that's it!

JACKIE Okay. Yeah. We got your share. If you wanna *call* it that.

(Beat.)

What's up, Shannon?

SHANNON What's *up*? What's *up*? I'll tell you what's *up*!! *(Glaring at THOMAS.)* I'm sick of people on this damn campus embracing our past! *Brainwashed* that God blesses the families of veterans! God does NOT bless the families of veterans.

THOMAS And how do you know that he doesn't??

SHANNON How do you know that he *does*?? Because your mommy told you?

THOMAS You watch your mouth!

SHANNON No, *you* watch *yours*!

SETH People!

THOMAS In fact, I'm beginning to really think that I don't want your stupid weed. I might just back out of all this.

JACKIE Don't say that!

SHANNON Is your conscience getting to you again, Thomas?

THOMAS What the hell does that mean??

SETH I'm beginning to think that this Humboldt trip is *really* a mistake.

JACKIE *(To SETH)* Don't say that!!

SHANNON You know exactly what it means!! You're paranoid. You don't know how to deal with smoking pot. Or with your mother finding out that you smoke pot.

SETH Shannon . . .

SHANNON I mean, isn't this all about *her*?? Isn't your mom some kind of a train wreck??

THOMAS *(Absolutely stunned.)* Whaa . . ?

SHANNON It's obvious. You don't what you are doing. One minute you're getting high, the next minute you're cutting back.

JACKIE Guys . . .

SHANNON One minute it's all fun and games, the next you're preaching family values.

SETH Shannon . . .

THOMAS You're so warped that you shout down anybody that disagrees with you!

SHANNON Whatever.

THOMAS And why don't you tell us what's going in on *your* family? Since you're so quick to point out *mine*!

SHANNON What??

THOMAS You heard me. What the hell is driving your freight train of anger? *Your* mother?

SETH Thomas!

THOMAS Your brother or sister?

SHANNON No.

THOMAS How about your *sick father?* Is it *him*?

(She slaps him. Big pause. Everybody gasps, stunned.)

JACKIE Whoa. Easy, guys.

SHANNON I'm . . . sorry.

THOMAS Save it.

SHANNON Thomas . . .

THOMAS Save it. *(Starts to exit.)*

SHANNON I didn't mean to do that. I . . .

THOMAS Whatever. *(Exits abruptly.)*

SHANNON Wow . . . what have I done? *(Puts her face in her hands, upset.)*

JACKIE Damn.

SETH Um. It's okay.

JACKIE You all right, Shannon?

SHANNON No. No, I'm not.

JACKIE Shazam. This is better than the movies.

SETH Jackie. Please.

JACKIE Well. I've got to go. Got a big computer date.

SETH *(Still focused on SHANNON.)* Have fun.

JACKIE Gonna be okay, girl?

SHANNON I'm fine.

JACKIE You sure?

SHANNON Yes. Just go.

JACKIE *(Starts to exit.)* Okay. Hey, be careful on the road. Lots of traffic this weekend. And check out Moe's in downtown Arcata, if you have time. I hear that it's a great little bar.

(Pause. SHANNON does not respond.)

Okay. I'll see you when you get back.

(She exits. Pause as he consoles SHANNON.)

SHANNON Can you believe I just did that?

SETH No. I can't.

(Pause.)

Look, you weren't the only one that lost your temper. Thomas was upset too. And honestly, he probably deserved what he got.

SHANNON Oh Seth, no he didn't! I didn't want to hit him! I didn't!

SETH I know . . . I know . . .

(Pause as they embrace each other. She is upset.)

SETH Look . . . I'm not gonna go into work. I'll just tell Lou something came up.

SHANNON No. Don't do that.

SETH I'm going to come with you.

SHANNON No.

SETH You shouldn't be going to Humboldt by yourself! It's over 300 miles away!

SHANNON No, Seth. You can't. You can't just *not* go to work at the last minute! They need you in there.

SETH Well . . .

SHANNON And aren't you late?

SETH No, no. It's not yet four o' clock. Almost.

SHANNON I'm going alone, Seth. I'll go and get this weed for everybody. And I really want to visit my cousin. That's the point of the whole trip for me. She and I are close.

SETH Yeah. I know. Well . . .

SHANNON And *then* I'm gonna go home. But thank you, though. I'm okay. The drive will be therapeutic. I need the time alone, to be honest.

SETH Do you?

SHANNON Yes. I really do.

(Beat.)

Hey . . . come here. Hold me. Hold me tight. *(They embrace.)* Not going to see you for a couple of days.

SETH It's just till tomorrow night.

SHANNON I know, I know. But still . . .

SETH But *still* . . .?

(Pause.)

Why do I feel like I'm not going to see you again?

SHANNON Be quiet and hold me, silly. You want me to slap you too?

SETH Ha. No.

SHANNON *(Pulling him closer.)* Come here. My little college boy . . .

SETH You're gonna make this college boy blush.

SHANNON Mmmmm. Always do. *(Kisses him, holds him close.)* That's right. My beautiful boy . . . with those North Stars.

SETH Um. That's me.

SHANNON Yep. *(Another kiss.)* My man.

SETH That's me. Oh. Hang on. Almost forgot. *(He pulls out the envelope of money, hands it to her.)* Here you go.

SHANNON What is it?

SETH Bay State's contribution to Humboldt's finest. Two-hundred dollars.

SHANNON Oh. Yeah. Sheesh. The money. *(Sticking it in pocket.)* Can't forget that.

SETH No, you can't. *(Kisses her. Beat.)* Well. I guess I need to get to work. Be careful. Lotta traffic this weekend, like Jackie said.

SHANNON Yeah. I'll be okay. *(She slowly pulls him to her for one more kiss)* One more . . . no two more.*(Kisses him again.)*

SETH *(Laughing)* I gotta go! It's four o' clock.

SHANNON Okay. I know.

SETH So . . .

SHANNON So . . .

SETH See you tomorrow night?

SHANNON *(Slowly)* Yeah. I'll see you tomorrow night.

SETH Bye!

(He quickly exits. Pause. SHANNON pulls off her backpack, sticks the envelope inside. She looks around, makes sure she is alone. Then she pulls out a pistol, quickly and discreetly. She opens the hatch, checks it, then closes it. She slowly takes practice aim at something, as if shooting at it. She puts the

gun back in the backpack, closes it up, and quickly exits.)

(Lights down. There is a long pause, and we hear something patriotic, the sounds of a snare drum that lead into a familiar American tune. We then hear a voice, formally announcing the names of several prominent physicists. A strobe light or a series of lights flash across the stage, and we see several elderly man standing or seated behind a lectern or a small table. If desired, this can be a video image quickly shown on the back wall. We hear the sounds of light applause, suddenly interrupted by gunfire. Several shots ring out, loudly, followed by screams and general mayhem. The chaos goes on for a few seconds, then gradually dies down. The last thing we hear is the waning music of the patriotic tune, diminishing with the light tapping of the snare drum. Then there is nothing. The stage is black. End of scene.)

SCENE FOUR

At RISE: The same evening. A small room on campus. A table and several chairs. As the lights go up, we see the DETECTIVE speaking with JACKIE and THOMAS. He/she is holding a pen and a small pad, taking notes. They are in the middle of a discussion. THOMAS's wig is lying on the table. As he has worked that night, Thomas is wearing a historical costume.

JACKIE Are we done yet?

DETECTIVE Excuse me?

JACKIE Are we finished?

THOMAS Exactly.

JACKIE We're not being charged with anything, are we?

DETECTIVE *Excuse me??* A friend of yours just shot two innocent people!

JACKIE Allegedly.

DETECTIVE Destroyed a lot of property! And then vanished! I'd say that's worth spending some time with me!

JACKIE *(Quietly.)* Okay.

(Pause.)

DETECTIVE Now. There's just a few more things.

THOMAS It's fine, sir. Go ahead.

DETECTIVE So . . . I know I've already asked you. But you two have *no* idea where Shannon might be headed? Where she might have gone?

THOMAS We don't. All we know is that she left town to go see a friend.

DETECTIVE That's where I need you to be specific. *What* friend?

JACKIE We don't know! She was very private about it. We told you, Shannon wasn't a close friend.

THOMAS Right. And she never said where it was. Or *who* it was. She just said she wanted to go see an old friend over the weekend.

DETECTIVE Hmmm. Was it family? Or was it a *friend?*

JACKIE *(Sighs.)* We told you. A *friend.* That's all she said.

THOMAS She was very private about her personal life. About her life away from Bay State.

DETECTIVE Was she . . . showing any signs of irrational behavior?

JACKIE Define irrational.

DETECTIVE I think you know what irrational means. Was she angry? Was she mad at anything?

THOMAS No. I don't think so.

JACKIE She wasn't like that.

THOMAS She was very calm and relaxed in general.

DETECTIVE Okay. *(Pause.)* Hmmpph.

THOMAS Yeah. Um. *(Looking right at the detective.)* She . . . she just wasn't the angry or emotional type. As far as I could tell. That just wasn't her.

(Pause. The DETECTIVE gives them a long look.)

DETECTIVE Okay. *(Sticks pad in his pocket.)* Okay. Well . . . that's it for now. You two be sure that you don't leave campus. Okay?

THOMAS We know.

JACKIE They told us.

DETECTIVE It's possible we'll have more questions for you later.

THOMAS All right.

(Pause. DETECTIVE turns to leave, sighs, gives them a long look.)

DETECTIVE Goodness. A girl goes psychotic and starts shooting at a bunch of unarmed, elderly men. Scientists, physicists. Patriots. People that did so much for country. I don't get it . . . *(He shakes his head and exits slowly.)* I just don't get it . . .

(He exits. Pause. JACKIE and THOMAS exchange long looks, relieved. THOMAS sits down, stunned.)

JACKIE People like him *never* get it.

THOMAS Wow. Jackie, what the hell happened tonight?

JACKIE I swear. What *did* happen?

THOMAS Shannon and I had a hard time getting on the same page. But I did not see *that* coming.

JACKIE Did, uh, Seth tell you?

THOMAS Tell me what?

JACKIE About the money. She put the money back in his backpack.

THOMAS Oh.

JACKIE She never took it. She was never going to Humboldt to begin with.

THOMAS Yeah, I know. He told me. *(Beat. He is still stunned.)* But . . . seriously. What the hell?? What did we just do? Did we allow . . . a murderer to get away?

JACKIE I don't know. I just want this night to be over.

THOMAS I just want this *summer* to be over.

JACKIE I know this isn't the best time to bring this up. But, damn! I was really looking forward to that weed!

(Pause.)

Right?

THOMAS Uh. Sure.

JACKIE That's it? *Sure??*

THOMAS Jackie . . .

JACKIE What?

THOMAS People almost died tonight. People were hurt.

JACKIE I know it. But still. I know you didn't put a lot of money towards it. But aren't you at least a little upset?

THOMAS Yeah. I know. The great *Humboldt marijuana.* But you know what else I know?

JACKIE You're not gonna start getting all weird, are you?

THOMAS All I know . . . is that people are more important than pot.

JACKIE Well. Of course.

THOMAS Human beings. Relationships. Mothers. Fathers.

(Pause.)

Families.

JACKIE Duhhh.

THOMAS Well, you *say* that. But Jackie, do you really *mean* it?? *(Stands up, begins to exit.)*

JACKIE What??

THOMAS You heard me.

JACKIE Whatever.

THOMAS I gotta go. Been a crazy day. I'm gonna go check on Seth. I wanna see what that detective asked him.

JACKIE Okay.

THOMAS Later.

(He exits. Pause. JACKIE is still puzzled.)

JACKIE *(Calls out.)* Of course I mean it! Why wouldn't I?? *(Pause. Calmly, to herself.)* Of course I mean it.

(She shrugs her shoulders and picks up the wig, plays with it. She then sits down and looks around carefully before lighting up a joint. She relaxes and smokes. She hums a tune similar to "Hail to the Chief" and twirls the wig. Lights fade to black.)

SCENE FIVE

At RISE: We hear the sounds of crickets in the background. A light goes up on stage left. SHANNON is at a roadside pay phone, holding the receiver, dialing a number. There is the sound of a ringing telephone as she waits. Lights up on stage right, a small table with a telephone, the back room of the campus café. Enter SETH, dressed in work clothes. He calls out to someone offstage as he enters, then picks up the receiver.

SETH *(Calling out)* Yeah! In the cooler. By the tomatoes. On the *middle* shelf! Not the top shelf! *(Picks up the ringing phone.)* Bay State Grill, can I help you?

SHANNON Hi Seth.

(Long pause. He is stunned.)

SETH Shannon . . . wow.

SHANNON Yeah. It's me.

SETH My God.

SHANNON Yep.

SETH Well. Um.

(Pause.)

Where are you?

SHANNON No *hi??* No *how have you been?*

SETH What . . . what are you doing? Where are you?

SHANNON Come on. You know that I can't tell you where I am. I'm . . . somewhere. I'm okay.

SETH So . . . um . . . I don't know what to say. You've been gone for two weeks. And *now* you decide to call??

SHANNON I know. I know.

(Pause.)

There are no words for what I did, Seth.

SETH There sure aren't. You shot two people. You put them in the hospital! And you . . . you lied to me! To all of us!

SHANNON I can't talk long, Seth. I know this phone line is being traced. But I know what I did. I know it wasn't honorable.

SETH It sure wasn't.

SHANNON I—

SETH But that doesn't stop me from missing you.

(Pause.)

SHANNON Do you?

SETH Yes.

SHANNON I absolutely miss you.

SETH Well . . .

SHANNON It's true.

SETH And so . . . now you're calling me.

SHANNON I didn't want to leave you, Seth. I didn't. And I don't know when you'll hear from me again. I'm out there, far away. I'll be out of the country within 48 hours.

SETH Wow.

SHANNON Yeah. I'm done with the nonsense. With the neutrons. For now.

(Pause.)

But . . . I had to tell you something . . .

SETH What is it?

SHANNON You were my whole world while I was at Bay State. My bedrock. My everything.

SETH No more . . . than what you were to me.

SHANNON You were all that I had in my short time there. And I know there was so much that I didn't tell you. So much.

SETH Shannon, look. You can work this out! You can work with the authorities. You can—

SHANNON No, Seth. What's done is done. I've chosen this path.

(Pause.)

I'm not looking for forgiveness. Or reconciliation. I'm looking . . . for something else.

SETH Yeah. I understand.

SHANNON Oh Seth . . . the evening sky here is gorgeous. It's so brilliant. I can see the North Star every night. I can see . . . the light of my summer boyfriend's eyes. Right here.

(Pause.)

Don't let the North Stars fade away. Don't let those beautiful things flame out. The world still needs a star to guide it.

SETH *(Musingly, sadly.)* The North Stars . . .

SHANNON That's right. The North Stars.

SETH Well . . . *you* don't let that crazy-ass girl go away for too long. The world is more interesting with you in it.

SHANNON Mmmm.

SETH Even if it might be more dangerous with you in it.

(Pause.)

Take care of yourself, Shannon. I'll be looking for you in the papers.

SHANNON Good-bye, Seth.

(They hang up. SHANNON looks left to right, then quickly steals away. Lights down on this part of the stage. SETH sits down, in quiet contemplation. Pause. Lights down on him. End of play.)

☞ More from Student Plays ☜

Othello's Just Another Fellow

Dramedy. **Grades 5-7.** 25-35 minutes. 8 actors: 4 males, 3 females, one teacher (or student portraying a teacher) 3 to 5 extras, if needed. ****A Latino-themed play****

A group of students are involved in a school production of *Othello*, but one of them is disturbed about the lack of diversity in the play. He takes certain steps to disrupt the play but in the end is encouraged by the others to try and make a difference in another, more constructive way. A lesson is learned, and the production is saved from disaster!

Pagasqueeny's Pantry

Comedy. **Middle/High School.** 15-20 minutes. 6 actors: 3 females, 2 males. One student (or a teacher) plays the comical role of the elderly Mr. Pagasqueeny.

Three friends sneak into Mr. Pagasqueeny's home to get something that one of them left behind. But in walks Pagasqueeny and they must hide in the pantry! In this comical play, a lesson is learned about honesty and trust, but it takes a heated discussion in the pantry and a subsequent attempt to escape to find this out!

Una Carta de Abuelo

Dramedy. **Middle/High School.** 35-45 minutes. 10 actors: 1 teacher, 5 females, 4 males. (With the option of 4-5 extra actors in two scenes.) ****A Latino-themed play****

Two cousins discover an old letter in their late grandfather's comic collection that they think leads to treasure! The cousins often butt heads, with one believing that he is more "Mexican," the other believing that some people make too much of a fuss about "being Mexican." Thus, they form their *own* groups in search of what Grandpa hid long ago. But what they find is actually worth more than merely silver or gold.

Barbecue at the Prom!

Dramedy. **Grades 5-8.** 25-35 minutes. 6 actors: 3 females, 3 males

It's a classic tale of guys versus girls! It's a prom committee, and everybody is supposed to work together but differences and opinions get in the way, causing the guys and girls to form their groups. For the end-of-the-year prom, one side wants pasta and lace, the other wants sports and barbecue! The two groups square off but eventually work together, demonstrating the importance of cooperation and compromise.

Going to Guatemala

Dramedy. **High School.** 50-60 minutes. 11 actors. 6 males, 5 females. ****A Latino-themed play****

A Latino student is chosen at the last minute to join a humanitarian group from his school that is headed to Guatemala. But since his Spanish is weak, he faces ridicule and criticism from certain peers. Jealousy and anger trickle throughout the campus as the trip approaches, and the social buzz of the high school becomes even more hectic when the student's trip money is stolen on campus, jeopardizing his trip.

Stravinsky's Kitchen

Comedy. **High School/College.** 12-15 minutes. 3 actors: 3 males (or females).

Two friends secretly enter the home of an employer to obtain a forgotten object but the homeowner abruptly arrives home while they are there. As they hide in the kitchen's pantry and plot their getaway, the two talk and eventually argue, exposing the true colors of one of them. Upon their hasty exit a mistake is made, and one of them capitalizes on this mistake, resulting in his/her fortune.

Forty Whacks

Drama. Spooky. **High School/College.** 25-35 minutes. 3 actors: 2 females, 1 male.

A pair of siblings have inherited the Lizzie Borden Bed and Breakfast in New England. Although the business was run for decades in a quiet, respectable fashion, one of the siblings is over-ambitious, wanting to unearth an alleged piece of buried evidence within the house. This brings about a chilly uneasiness between brother and sister, and perhaps within the house itself.

John Calhoun and a Thief

Drama. **College.** 35-40 minutes. 3 actors: 2 females, 1 male.

Kicked out of a university PhD program, a bitter and dejected female lifts from the library archives original copies of John Calhoun's personal documents. Counseled and consoled by her roommates, her conscience slowly gets to her; but as she seeks entry to other universities her luck turns to worse, and the subsequent decisions she makes regarding the historic papers cause this one-act play to become darker, if not funnier.

Honoring the Hijacker

Drama. **College.** 12-15 minutes. 4 actors: 2 females, 2 males.

It's 1981, the ten-year anniversary of the famed hijacker D.B. Cooper. The play's four characters are attending a "D.B. Festival" and have stayed up very late, outlasting everybody else. The late night chit-chat goes from pranks and jokes to outright volatility, and suddenly this get-together becomes something that three of the four characters didn't bargain for.

It's a Super Day at Sammy's!

Comedy. **Middle or High School.** 35-40 minutes. 9 actors: 5 females, 4 males (4 possible adults).

Jodi has found a summer job at a travel agency. But her three younger siblings can't seem to live without her! They call her at the office incessantly, which interferes with the work. The standard telephone greeting "It's a super day at Sammy's!" becomes a repeated theme of this comedy, as Jodi struggles to reach a balance between her job and her nagging siblings

Three Tenners

Comedy/Drama. **Elementary through High School.** Three Ten-Minute Plays.

Three Creepy Plays

Drama. **Middle School through College.** Three short 'creepy' plays.

Hockey Masks in Hueytown

Drama. Spooky. **High School/College.** 20-25 minutes. 4 actors: 2 males, 2 females.

Driving home for Thanksgiving break, four college students stop off in a small rural town to retrieve one of the student's old family pictures. They reluctantly enter the empty home of his deceased uncle, a former producer for the Friday the 13th movies. Strange objects are found during their search . . but when a hockey mask surfaces, everything really goes sideways.

The Witch Makes Five

Drama. Spooky. **High School.** 10 minutes. 4 actors: 2 males, 2 females.

After a bizarre group camping trip, a student is checked into a youth mental facility . When she is visited by the other members of the trip, memories of the weekend trickle out . . . and horrific things begin to happen.

Mrs. Calapooza and the Culebra

Dramedy. **Grades 5-8.** 10 minutes. 5 actors: 3 females, 2 males.

Fed up with their grouchy teacher's classroom ways, four students complain and bicker back and forth during a Spanish quiz. The situation grows worse when the friends discover that one of them has pulled the ultimate prank on the teacher.

Raiders of the Lost Rakasa

Dramedy. **Grades 5-8.** 10 minutes. 7 actors: 4 females, 3 males.

Seven young explorers arrive at a cave in a far-off land in search of the great "Rakasa." They find what they want . . . along with a few of the cave's unexpected surprises.

www.ingramcontent.com/pod-product-compliance
Lightning Source LLC
Chambersburg PA
CBHW071928020426
42331CB00010B/2772

* 9 7 8 0 9 9 8 8 5 2 3 3 1 *